THE ONE-WOMAN SHOW

THE ONE-WOMAN SHOW

Monodramas

BY

MARJORIE MOFFETT

WITH A FOREWORD BY

DANIEL FROHMAN

SAMUEL FRENCH

NEW YORK LOS ANGELES

SAMUEL FRENCH LTD. LONDON

1935

PRINTED IN THE UNITED STATES OF AMERICA
BY THE VAIL-BALLOU PRESS, INC., BINGHAMTON, N. Y.

To

DANIEL FROHMAN,

beloved "Uncle Dan" to the people of the theatre

FOREWORD

BY DANIEL FROHMAN

An introduction is sometimes necessary, both for an artist and for a book.

So I introduce Marjorie Moffett and her sketches. And I do so heartily and with pleasure, for I am personally acquainted with her great and splendid gifts as a dramatic and picturesque *diseuse,* whose performances are filled with humor and pathos.

So, too, with these sketches, which are the framework of those performances. Each is a dramatic epitome of character—the tragic ones disturbingly beautiful and the comic ones gay and diverting. Always they give a vivid glimpse of varied life—sure to amuse and please.

Marjorie Moffett lifts the monologue to the field of art. To those of us who have seen these sketches come to life under the magic of her touch they will have especial appeal. But to everyone they should prove interesting and amusing reading.

CONTENTS

PAGE

New York—1934 3

As It Probably Was—Lady Godiva (After the Ride 11

Mrs. Tuttle-Adams in Politics . . . 19

"Mrs. Tuttle-Adams Speaking" . . . 27

Ladies of the Chorus 37

Dedicating the Potsville Open Air Theatre 45

Little Italy 51

Bargain Basement 57

Introducing Shropsy-Topsy—A Department Store Rhapsody 67

A Cheerful Earful 73

An English Lady's Impressions of America 79

A Philadelphia Mother Visits School . 93

A Debutante at a Country Club Dance . 101

Vera Cheera's Morning Sunshine Talk 109

L'Espionne 117

NEW YORK—1934

NEW YORK—1934

Oh, Mrs. Elliott! Mrs. Elliott, are you up? This is Jennie. Oh, Mrs. Elliott, I'm sorry to bother you but I have to get out early and mom's still asleep. I wanted to ask you if you'd run in and sit with her later. She had another bad night and I worry about leaving her. Oh, I don't know how to thank you, Mrs. Elliott. You've been so kind. And—and there's something else. I—I hate to ask you but we're all out of coffee. Would you lend me just enough for her breakfast until I can get some and—and fix it for her? I'll get a job today I know. Oh, thank you. Oh, no, thanks, I'll get some breakfast later. I can't stop now. I have to rush if I'm going to get a job. Thank you, Mrs. Elliott. Thank you awfully much. Good-bye.

Dear God, help me. Don't make me have to go to charity. I couldn't do it, God. Don't You know I couldn't do it? I'd kill myself first. But there's mom and there isn't anything left to eat, God. There isn't anything left to eat. "Seek and ye shall find." That's in Your Book, God. I am seeking but show me where. Show me *where,* God.

Hello, Charlie. Fine, thanks. Yes, a *Tribune,* please. Oh, no! No, I forgot. I forgot, Charlie; I'm sorry. I've got a job and I don't need a paper this morning! I mean I won't have time to read it! Yes, isn't that funny? Force of habit, I guess.

Now, why did I say that? Why didn't I tell him the truth? Why didn't I tell him I didn't even have three cents in my purse, instead of lying like that just to save my face? That's what's the matter with me. Pride. I need to have it taken out of me before I'll deserve a job. And how will I ever get one when I haven't even a paper to look up the want ads? I'd better put my pride in my pocket, since I've nothing else there, and go back and ask him if he'll trust me for it. He knows I'm honest—he'll— No. No, I can't. I just told him I had a job. Maybe I'll find a paper that someone's thrown down. I can pick it up without anyone's noticing. There I go again! Why should I be too proud to pick up a paper when I haven't even three cents to my name to buy one? There's one now on top of that rubbish can! I'll pick it up whether anyone's looking or not. Who do I think I am anyway—not wanting to pick up a paper? Now . . . let's see. Oh, I hope they left the Help Wanted Section in it! Here's part of it. . . . "Stenographer wanted—excellent opportunity . . . must know French and German." . . . Oh, why didn't I study that instead of four years of Latin? "Switchboard operator—scrubwoman—seamstress"—I might try that. . . . Here's something! . . . "Young woman wanted—folding letters—addressing envelopes—no experience necessary"—that's for me all right! "210 West 12th Street"—Oh, God, how can I get there with no carfare? It will take hours to walk it from here and someone will have it by that time. Still it may be just a test. It may be fate. I've got to try it. I'll walk very fast. Dear God, please keep that job open until I get there . . . please keep that job open until I get there . . . please keep that job open. . . .

Oh, God, what now? My shoe! The sole is thru! I knew it couldn't last much longer. Forty-eighth. Thirty-six blocks yet to go! If I could just stick some cardboard in it—I know—I'll stop in this doorway and put in some of this newspaper—several thicknesses. . . .

"Wednesday! July 18th!" Yesterday's paper! Oh, God, how could I ever have been so blind as not to notice! Fifty-eight blocks already to follow up a job advertised in yesterday's paper! That's a laugh these days. These days with a hundred people clamoring for every job before the ink is even dry on the paper! God, You must be laughing at me. How You must be laughing at me! Oh, God, please, please listen. There's mom. She's depending on me, God. Oh, I know I was a fool not to have looked at the date on that paper! It was just because I was feeling so dizzy this morning. My brain won't work any longer. I'm ready to give up. I'm scared! I'm scared, God! I haven't any pride left any longer. I feel so—funny. Maybe I could get my courage back if I just had a cup of coffee. . . .

Oh! Oh, no, thank you. I'm—I'm all right. I just felt a little dizzy for a minute. I—I guess it's the heat. I'm all right now. Thank you. Thank you very much. Oh, yes, I had breakfast. Thank you, I'm not hungry—that is, I'm not *very* hungry. I've—I've just been walking a long way. I'm—I'm looking for a job and I—I haven't any money. You will? You mean—in this restaurant? Oh! Oh, of course, I don't care what I do! Of course, I can wait table! And I can wash dishes and scrub! I'm very strong and quick and I'll work very hard! You won't be sorry. Nights? Oh, I don't mind! I'll work day and night—eighteen hours a day —I don't care! I'll show you how grateful I am! Ten dollars a week and my meals? Oh, of course, it's satisfactory! It's wonderful! May I start right away? Yes, I'd like to. Well, I could take just a bowl of soup, if you've plenty, and then I'll start right in. Thank you. You're very kind. Only—only would you let me use your telephone for just a minute first? I—I want to tell my mother so she won't worry any more. I'll—I'll pay you back for the call as soon as I get my salary. Thank you.

Hello. Give me Trafalgar 7-7439. Oh, God, thank You! Thank You, God. You were looking out for us, after all, weren't You? Oh, God, it feels so good to have a job—so good. Hello, Mrs. Elliott? Mrs. Elliott, this is Jennie. Would you do me a great favor? Would you mind telling my mother I've found a *job?* Thank you, Mrs. Elliott. Thank you very much.

AS IT PROBABLY WAS—LADY GODIVA (AFTER THE RIDE)

AS IT PROBABLY WAS—LADY GODIVA (AFTER THE RIDE)

Well, thank heaven, *that's* over. I wish I'd had a cushion on that saddle! Alfrieda, for heaven's sake, make me a cocktail. I'm perishing.

Did I have a nice ride? Are you being sarcastic? Just remember, Alfrieda, I have ridden today to save a nation. Men shed blood, Alfrieda, but I shed clothes! Give me the papers. Have any messages come? Well, there should be some. I sent several myself—purely congratulatory ones, of course. I wanted the Earl to see that it had met with the proper response. Well, don't stand there looking like a penguin. Give me the papers. UMMMMMMM. "Lady Godiva Goes Off the Clothes Standard—Blonde Takes Wild Ride."

There's someone now. Maybe it's the boy with the messages.

Why, Leofric—you back so soon? I thought you were hunting and wouldn't be home until dinner. Why, what in the world is the matter, dear? Why, Leo, you don't mind, do you? After all, it was your idea, you know. Oh, Leofric, don't be so prudish, dear. One would think I was in the *habit* of going around undressed!

Just look at all this publicity. I've made the front page of every paper in town.

Why, Leofric, what a perfectly vile thing to say to your wife! "Riding naked all over town," indeed! A nice way to talk about my sacrifice! You're just as crude as mother always said you were. If I were like some of the women in our set, you might have cause to complain. You ought to see the way Lucretia dresses ever since she came back from the city. Heavens, you can see right thru her and here we thought she was going to be a missionary!

Really, Leofric, you're impossible. You suggest something and I do it, hoping to impress you, and you astonish me by being peevish about it. You'd better take a dose of that herb remedy. Your liver must be out of order.

Leofric, are you trying to get out of keeping your promise? Well, that's what it looks like. But you needn't think you can get away with it. Everyone in Coventry knows the condition under which, as well as in which, I rode this afternoon and you can't back out of it now.

Well, how was I to know you were exaggerating? I thought, of course, that you were in deadly earnest and I never dreamed that you would suggest something that you wouldn't want me to do.

Why, I did nothing of the sort. How can you say that? And you needn't say that I started just as soon as your back was turned. You had been gone nearly an hour. I had all my housekeeping accounts to go over first and order the dinner and, what with one thing and another, it was noon before I got started. Anyway, I didn't go so far—just down the main street.

Well, I started in just above the meat market and kept on down past the feed store until I came to the old ice house. Then I turned at the square and came on back. There was practically no one about. I took the precaution of asking everyone to stay inside with the shutters closed. I can see no occasion for your getting so upset. Practically no one saw me.

Don't be absurd, Leofric. You can't see thru shutters. And, if you could, I'd like to know what wise cracks anyone could make about *my* figure. Thank goodness, I'm as slim as ever. I must say that eighteen day diet—

Leofric, if you must use such language, I'll have to ask you to go to the club. I simply can't have it in the house. I have enough trouble with the servants as it is. Heavens, anyone would gather from your manner that I'd gone out and had an affair with someone.

Now, you needn't get sarcastic, Leofric. I'm no more enterprising than other women. It's all in your mental attitude. At least, you must give me credit for following your suggestions.

Well, what if poor Tom did peep? I don't see any harm in that. It probably wouldn't be the first time that he'd seen the figure of a woman. There are plenty of statues in the museum he might have looked at, even if he'd never seen a live one. You just have one of those suspicious minds, Leo, and think that what is art in a museum is indecency in your own wife. Anyway, it's not my responsibility. It was your idea and, as far as I'm concerned, the incident is closed.

Leofric dear, you're your own worst enemy, really you are. If you'd just make up your mind that this was done with the best and purest of motives and think of it that way, why, then everything would be all right. Mark my words, Leo. Years from now, if someone rides on horseback to save his country, they'll make a hero out of him! Well, what if he will be dressed? That's merely a technicality.

What is it, Alfrieda? Messages? Such a lot of them. I wonder who they can be from.

UMMMMM. Just listen to this, Leo, if you think I've been such a fool! "Pool's, the choice of royalty the world over, wishes to add you to the list of their distinguished clients." I guess that will put you in your place. "We are sending you special jars of Pool's two creams for your dressing table, engraved with your family crest. Please send pictures of yourself, castle and dressing table. Also of horse, if possible." Leo, do you realize that this is the most important thing that could possibly happen to me? Only the cream of society ever receives such an invitation! Heaven knows, I had no idea of personal gain when I agreed to sacrifice myself and thought only of the good of the people but I can see now that, after having been in the public eye—figuratively speaking, of course, I mean—it may be the beginning of a career. Here's another one. "We offer you five thousand dollars to run full page color advertisement of yourself and horse, the first of our new series, "Nature in the Raw." Leo, it *is* the beginning of a career! Now you can just tell those loafers in the square that, "He laughs best who laughs last," as we say up here in Coventry!

Oh, don't be so impetuous, darling. You know perfectly well that I was only thinking of you, as I always do. After all, now that you won't have the added income from this tax, I feel that I should do what I can to help out. Heaven knows, I don't want to be one of those useless, clinging vine sort of creatures. I think they should be exterminated. I'm going right out and answer these now.

Leofric, don't you dare start to argue with me. You know how it always prostrates me—especially after the emotional strain I have just been under. And, for heaven's sake, don't look so disgruntled. Anyone would think I'd had an affair with someone. Just remember, Leo, that my only company on that ride was the horse!

Alfrieda, where on earth is that cocktail?

MRS. TUTTLE-ADAMS IN POLITICS

MRS. TUTTLE-ADAMS IN POLITICS

Hello. Hello. Plaza 3–4873. Plaza 3–4873. Goodness, operator, what's the matter? It's just around the corner.

Hello. Hello. Let me speak to Mrs. Musgrave, please. Yes. This is Mrs. Tuttle-Adams speaking. Mrs. *Tuttle-Adams.* T-u-double t-l-e HYPHEN Capital A—d-a-m-s. How do you suppose you spell it? What? Nonsense! Of course, she's in! Why did you ask who's calling if she's out? Oh, well, tell her it's Mrs. Adams and I want to talk to her at once.

Hello. Hello, Daisy! Certainly it's I. Well, I've just decided to use my full name. I think it sounds so much better that way, don't you? Well, I don't think a woman should lose her identity completely just because she's married. Besides, Tuttle is such a distinguished name. My dear, I just met the Republican candidate and he's such a sweet man. I'm going to vote for him too.

Just a minute, Daisy. Excuse me, dear. There's someone at the door.

Yes, come in. Oh, good-morning, Miss Butler. I'm so glad you're early, for there's so much to attend to and I'm just a wreck this morning. You'd better begin by retyping my speech. I rewrote the whole thing last night.

Excuse me, Daisy. Miss Butler just came in. We're working on my speech. I call it, "Are Women Meeting Their Political Challenge?"

Twilight! Twilight! Put it down, darling. Put it down, sir. Do you hear me? Go over to your pillow and lie down.

Excuse me, Daisy. Twilight was just being mischievous.

Well, Daisy, I wanted to ask you about the meeting this afternoon. What are you wearing? Oh, heavens, don't do that! Well, I'm wearing red and we'd clash. Well, I always feel that red suggests hospitality, don't you?

Twilight! Twilight! Don't DO that, darling. Now be mumsie's nice doggie.

Excuse me, Daisy. What were you saying? Yes. Yes, I think that would be lovely. Wear that, by all means.

Just a minute, Daisy. Excuse me, dear. There's someone at the door again.

Yes. Come in. Oh, good-morning, Jane.

Who? The caterer? Oh, heavens, I'd forgotten all about him!

Miss Butler, will you go downstairs and see to him please? Be especially sure about the ice cream please. I ordered it all in the forms of brown derbies—*brown derbies*—you know HATS—the emblem of the Democratic party—and I asked them to let me see a sample early, for I didn't want the added mental strain of not being sure it was all right. Yes. Thank you. That's all.

Oh, yes, Daisy. I'm so sorry, dear, but I can't help these interruptions. What was I saying? Oh, yes, I knew there was something I'd forgotten. I wanted to tell you about Mr. Tuttle—the Republican candidate, you know. I met him yesterday and we may be related. We have the same name, you know. My dear, he's such a sweet man, so I'm going to support the Republicans too.

Well, my dear, I don't see what difference that makes. Well, I know I'm on the Democratic committee but, after all, I think we should all work together, don't you?

Oh, politics—politics—politics! I just adore it!

Why, certainly, I know what his platform is. Don't you think I read the newspapers? Daisy, don't be an idiot. What if I am a member of the Democratic committee? Is that any reason why I can't work for the Republicans too? I'm also a member of the W. C. T. U. Well, I think we should all be broadminded about those things—like the Community Fund. That's the only way we can progress.

Twilight! Don't do that, darling.

Oh, Daisy, don't be absurd. Mr. Tuttle may be a relation. Well, of course, I don't know positively but I'm sure he must be and blood is always thicker than whatever it is.

Well, Daisy, when he's practically a relation, I can do no less than support him. Well, I always believe in giving the benefit of the doubt. Oh, Daisy, don't be absurd. Why should it be embarrassing? I'll simply tell them when they arrive that I've changed my mind. After all, it's a free country. That's every person's privilege.

Daisy, why on earth shouldn't I change my mind if I want to? Even Al Smith does that. Certainly he does. He's practically deserted New York and he's running for Governor in New Jersey. Why, certainly, I know. It was in the paper. Don't you ever read the papers? Oh, Daisy, you just skim over the headlines the way so many do. You don't really analyze the situation. Daisy, don't be an idiot. Don't I know the man? Well, I shook hands with him once in Albany. Well, I know it was a long time ago but I did it.

Well, anyway, he was over in Patterson or Stamford or some place over there and he said you couldn't run a hot dog stand the way New Jersey was being run. The governor there is only part time and Al Smith says it's terrible. Well, you don't have to believe me if you don't want to. I tell you I saw it. He's going to run for governor full time and I'm certainly going to vote for him. Oh, Daisy, don't be so technical. What if I do live in New York? Don't be so provincial. I just as soon vote in one state as another.

Oh, Daisy, don't be absurd. Of course, they must come. Why on earth shouldn't they? We'll go right on with the program just the same. Daisy, is there any reason why, just because I've turned Republican, I shouldn't have a Democratic committee meeting in my house? We can talk for both sides and let them take their choice. That's the only fair way to do anyway. I've got my whole speech rewritten along those lines.

Oh, Daisy, don't be so partial. It's very small of you, dear. You mustn't have such a one channel mind. Just wait until you see the ice cream and you'll believe I'm a good Democrat, even if I have turned Republican.

Oh, yes, I knew there was something I'd forgotten. There'll probably be some argument afterward. You know how those women are. So I want you to sanction everything I say—about working for both sides and all that, I mean. Now, Daisy, don't argue. I've given my word and you've got to keep my promise.

Well, come over early, dear, and we'll talk it over. I've got to go down and see the caterer now. Between you and him, I feel like those poor Chinese—attacked on every front.

Good-bye, darling. Good-bye. See you this afternoon.

Jane! Jane, tell the caterer to wait. I want to see him personally. And, Jane! Tell him I've changed my mind about the ice cream! I want to have a special mold made—an elephant wearing a brown derby!!

"MRS. TUTTLE-ADAMS SPEAKING"

"MRS. TUTTLE-ADAMS SPEAKING"

Jane! Jane, answer the phone and, if it's that reporter from the SUN, tell him I'll call him back in an hour. I simply can't make my voice vibrant so early in the morning.

Who? Mrs. Musgrave? Oh, heavens, give it to me!

Hello, Daisy. How are you, darling? Oh, I'm a wreck. I never closed my eyes the entire night. Well, I was working on my speech of welcome, you know, and, when my creative forces are at work, I simply cannot sleep. But the speech is a masterpiece. I begin it, "Justice! Justice! E pluribus unum!" Don't you think that's well expressed, Daisy? I just adore those old epithets at a time like this. Well, I don't know exactly *what* it means—like everyone else I never can exactly understand dear Mr. Browning—but it seems to put everything in a nutshell, don't you think so?

I was just going to call you up to ask about your paper. You know, if I have some idea of the length and style of the various numbers, I can tell better how to arrange the program.

Twilight! Twilight! Put it down, darling. Put it down, sir. Do you hear me? Go over to your pillow and lie down.

No, Daisy. No, dear. I wasn't talking to you. Twilight chose to chew up my best gold boudoir slipper and I had to reprimand him. Certainly he understands. He's a very sensitive dog—you ought to see his pedigree. Why, if that dog could talk, he wouldn't speak to either one of us!

Well, what's the paper about, Daisy? Oh, yes, yes, the Balkan conference! Ah, la belle Balkan—la belle—you know, after being in Paris for nearly two months, I have the greatest difficulty in not talking French to everyone!

You know, we met King Boris over there. He's a darling—so virile—altho not so much as Mussolini. My dear, *there's* the most divine man! He reminds me of Valentino. He flashed thru the Corso—or is it the Torso? I never can remember.

Twilight! Twilight! Don't *do* that, darling. Be mumsie's nice doggie.

Excuse me, Daisy. What were you saying? Oh, yes. Well, where's the conference being held, Daisy? What? It's *over?* Oh, is it? Well, where was it? Athens? My dear, what a divine place for a conference, with all the ruins and everything.

You know, it's going to be an awfully absorbing program. I simply can't wait for it. You know, that new Mrs. Hicks is going to be there. Yes. Yes, I invited her this morning—had an awfully interesting talk with her about Russia. Oh, no; no, she isn't from there. She's from Connecticut but that doesn't matter. She thinks Russia's the neighboring state. Oh, yes, you know her. She's the chairman of some committee or other for the Uplift Society. I'm working for her on it. I don't know just what it's for but I'm on it. Well, I don't know how to describe her to you—sort of nondescript. She's the kind who could have seventeen children by a man and never call him anything but Mr. Hicks.

Twilight! Twilight! GO OVER TO YOUR PILLOW AND LIE DOWN! Now don't let me have to speak to you again.

Excuse me, Daisy. Twilight was just being mischievous.

Oh, yes, about the paper. I must make notes so as to know how and where to introduce you.

Let's see. Is Bulgaria in Jugo-Slavia? Oh, no, of course not. It's Czecho Slovakia I was thinking of. How frightfully stupid of me to ask! I know that perfectly well, for we had so much Early American glassware given us for wedding presents and I remember Wesley saying that Czecho Slovakia must be in a fair way to pay off the national debt from what was wished on us when we got married. Or maybe it was Serbia. I've forgotten which. One of those *Asiatic* countries, anyway. Well, anyhow it doesn't matter.

You know, I feel keenly that the time I spent studying geography was just wasted with Europe all laid out in a new pattern now. I never have felt quite right about their deliberately tearing the place all up and making it over to suit themselves. I always say you sort of expect mathematics and history to change but a town should stay in the same country, don't you think so?

Ah, "Pax Vobiscum!" That's an old saying from the French, Daisy. It means, "We're here today and gone tomorrow."

Oh, no, please go on. I'm terribly interested. You know, I never knew before that Jugo meant south. That's really important, isn't it?

I'm so glad you brought out that point, for I suppose nearly everybody thinks as I did that it meant some kind of a religious sect.

Twilight, put that down, darling. Now, don't let me have to speak to you again. Now, don't feel so badly, darling. It hurts me much worse than it does you when I have to reprimand you.

Yes, Daisy. How many did you say? Why, what on earth do they all do? But I suppose they just live on rice and rats like the Chinese. Really, Daisy, you're marvelous. I don't see how you ever find out so much about everything over there. You must read the ATLANTIC MONTHLY and the NATIONAL GEOGRAPHIC and all the rest of them. Oh, yes, I take them too. I always have. I pride myself on keeping up on everything. I think we should, don't you? I think it's terrible when a woman lets herself go and doesn't let her mind progress. That's what I always say to myself, "Keep your mind working along national issues. Let it progress. Don't stagnate. Fight stagnation. Progress." That's my motto.

Twilight! Stop scratching that way!

You know, Daisy, I'm worried about him. He doesn't seem well and I take him to the veterinary every week and wash him in Lux regularly every day and keep him properly brushed and never allow him to associate with common dogs a tall. I don't understand it.

Why, of *course,* I'm interested, Daisy. How can you think otherwise? Here I'm just taking notes and planning the best way to introduce you. Would you rather open the program or close it?

Oh, yes, I *knew* there was something I wanted to tell you! Wesley said that Bulgaria is only about the size of Toledo—or maybe it was Indianapolis—I've forgotten which. That's very interesting, don't you think so? You might put that in. Oh, you know, I should think Princess Giovanna would hate it, wouldn't you? Imagine having to live in a small town like Bulgaria after Rome! Oh, dear old Rome! I simply adore it! I've never been there but I just adore it!

What? Oh, my dear, is there more? What? An hour and twenty minutes? Well, my dear, I suppose I heard the salient part of it. You know, I'm wondering if Twilight could possibly have a flea. I don't see how he could but he's scratching so that it worries me.

You know, those people from downstairs were up on the roof this morning when I had him up. They have a Boston bull but they're from Seattle and I just wondered if he could have caught something. Oh, yes, you know them. She's blonde with a mole on her nose. Yes, that's the one! Their name is Upright, I remember, for, when she told me, I asked her immediately if they were the ones who manufactured the pianos but I forgot whether she said they did or didn't. Anyway, they're from Duluth or Seattle. I've forgotten which—someplace down south, anyway, and I shouldn't be a tall surprised if their dog had fleas—so many darkies, you know. No. No. Twilight was on the other side of the roof; we called across to them. I never allow him to associate with common dogs. You know that, Daisy. But those things are in the air, you know. I'm sure he has them. You will excuse me, won't you, Daisy? I'm terribly interested in the paper and thanks for telling me about it in advance. It will help me so much in arranging the program but I must go now and give poor Twilight his bath. Good-bye, darling. Good-bye. See you this afternoon and I simply can't wait to hear the paper. Good-bye.

Jane! Jane! Fill Twilight's tub at once and bring me the box of Lux.

Twilight, come to mumsie, darling. Did nassy ole fleas get on Twilight from nassy ole common doggie? Well, his mumsie'll fix 'em ole fleas, yes, she will. . . .

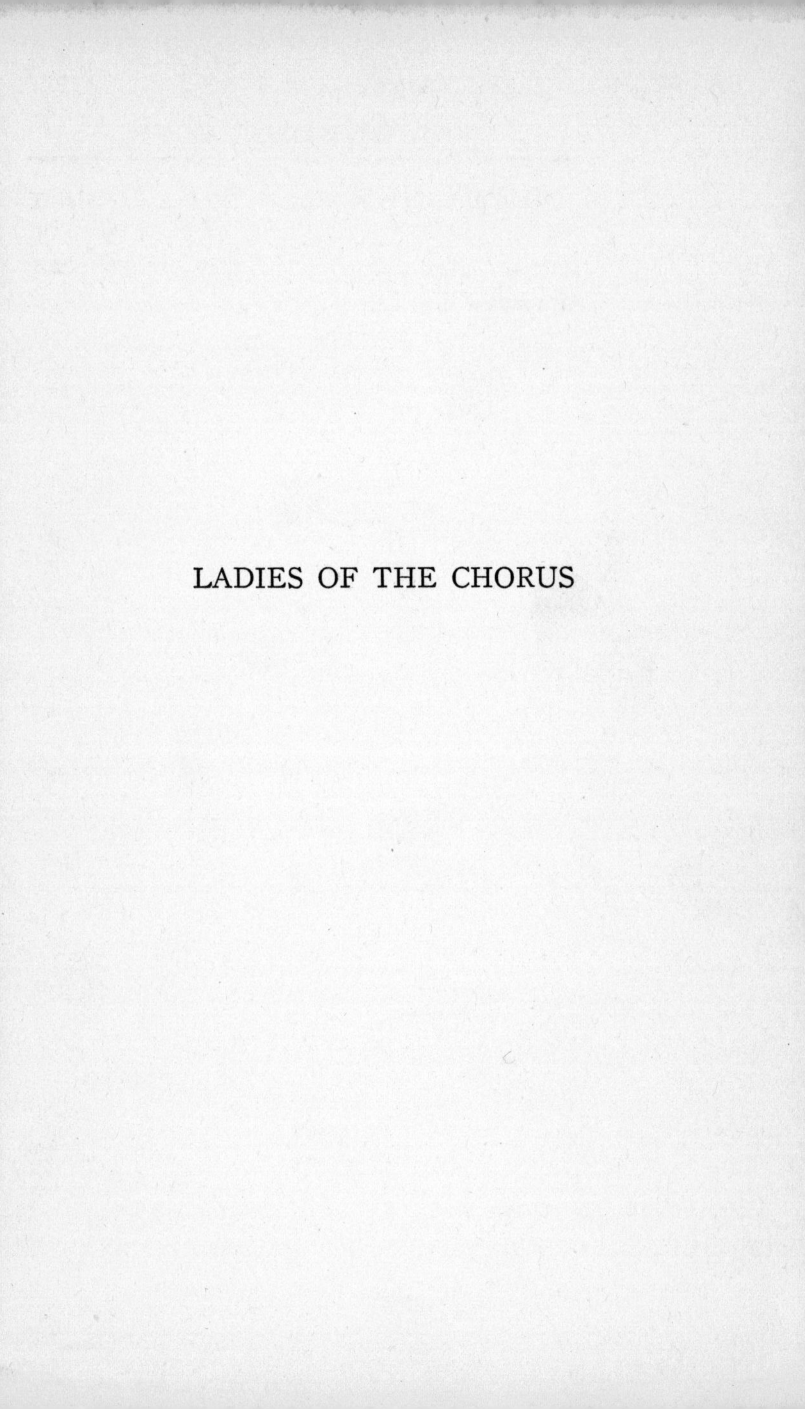

LADIES OF THE CHORUS

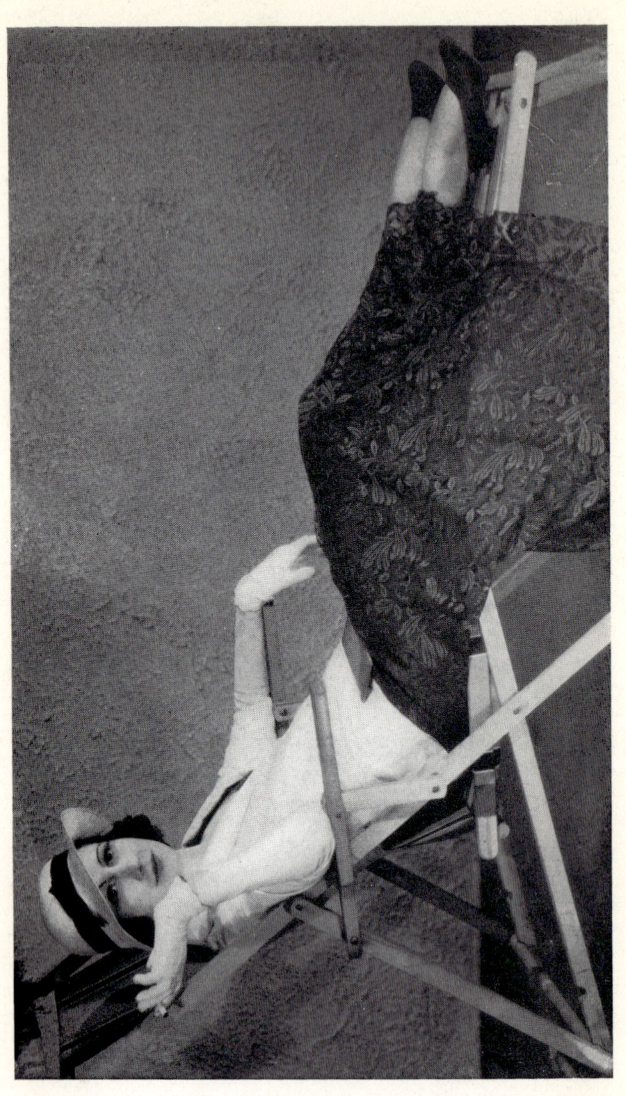

LADIES OF THE CHORUS

Dotty! What on earth are you doing down here? Well, of all things! How perfectly fascinating to run into you! And just when I was getting so tired of being down here alone that I was ready to pack up and go back to town. Come on. Sit down and let's talk. Oh, no! I forgot! I *cawn't* sit down. Well, I got sunburned yesterday and now I have to stand up all the time. Oh, I went to sleep lying face down on the beach. You can imagine the rest. I even have to stand up to eat.

Say, you must be doing all right to be able to come down here. Whom is he? The same one? Well, at least, he's faithful and that's more than you can say for most of them.

Oh, I don't think you know mine. He's a new one—in the plumbing business. From Phily, thank God, so he only comes over twice a week.

At the Waldorf? Saaay, you *are* doing all right. Oh, I got an apartment on 72nd Street but I'm moving down to the east side as soon as I get back to town. I cawn't stand it up there any more. The neighborhood's all shot. I guess there's hardly a decent woman on the block. I told Pinky he certainly couldn't expect me to live in such surroundings, so he's rented me a penthouse on Park Aaavenue. Gorgeous old English setting and all that sort of thing. Pinky just dotes on everything English—especially since he learned to speak it.

Oh, his name's Pincus—Montmorency Pincus. I call him Pinky for short. Oh, the usual kind—about fifty-five. He tells me he won't be forty until April! Well, I must say he's very good to me. He gives me everything I can get out of him. He loves me more than anything in the world, but, of course, he's gotten sort of attached to his wife and children *too*.

No, I haven't seen a decent man in the place but, of course, I only came down yesterday and, as I say, I got so sunburned that last night I didn't feel like looking around. Besides, Pinky's coming down tonight, so I got to be careful. He gets furious if I so much as look at another man.

Whom? Fred? Really? You know, the lawst time I run into Fred he was out on a big bust with a coupla hairdressers from the Savoy

Plaza. And after I'd been practically faithful to him for two months! You know, his father paid me ten thousand dollars never to see him again. Yeah. You know, a thing like that sort of gives you back your faith in men, don't it?

Oh, sure, I guess I'll go back. Pinky don't want me to, of course, but I tell him I cawn't afford to give up my career, so long as he don't give up his family. Besides, just between you and I, this game is not what it used to be. I wanted a new car but Pinky didn't come across. He says the plumbing business is all shot.

Oh, gee, it seems good to get away from it all—out here in the country where you can get your feet on good old terra cotta, don't it? Nature is always so natural, don't chew think so? The sea is always the sea—no pretense. Say, don't that view over there make you think of that first act set in *Rio Rita?*

Well, look who's coming, Dot! A coupla Rotarians from Cedar Rapids coming over to give the little girls a break!

No, thanks, big shots; if I wanted a chair, I'd sit down in this one. Also, we didn't just get in from Sinking Springs and we don't believe the Easter bunny lays hard boiled eggs. So beat a retreat.

Wouldn't it take somebody with a Jack Gilbert smile on a Laurel and Hardy face to try to pull something like that? Look at 'em in the back, will ya? As if they weren't bad enough from the front without wishing the rear on us!

Well, at least, the days when turning down a possible dinner date meant having to heat up a can of beans over the gas jet are over—for both of us.

Jimmy? No? Did you, Dot?

What? Look out for what? Sunburn? Oh! Oh, that's better now. Besides, I'm tired, and want to sit down.

Listen, Dot, how is he? Does he ever ask about me? Oh, I suppose I always will feel that way about him. Funny, ain't it—how there's always one man who can sort of get you going, no matter what he done to you?

Gee, I just had my fortune told yesterday and the fortune teller told me I was going to see him again. I went back today just to see if she'd tell me the same thing. Funny, ain't it, how you sort of clutch hold of a coupla wet tea leaves to try to make you believe what you want to believe?

Well, she didn't exactly mention his name but she said I was goin' to a party and every man

I'd ever known was goin' to be there. I said, "My God, they'll have to hire Radio City!"

Dotty!!!! Oh, no, it's just my darned imagination. Gee, for a minute—just talking about him—I thought that was Jimmy over there. Oh, I guess it will always be that way with me. I guess when you want a person so bad you start seein' him every place you go. You sort of carry him with you, I guess.

Gee, seein' you has got me all upset. Come on! I'd better snap out of this. Pinky'll be here tonight!

DEDICATING THE POTSVILLE OPEN AIR THEATRE

DEDICATING THE POTSVILLE OPEN AIR THEATRE

Dear Friends of Potsville: As chairman of the Potsville Dedication Committee, I am very happy to welcome you, my dear fellow citizens of Potsville, not forgetting our dear friends from the adjacent cities, who have come to help celebrate this occasion, to this beautiful open air theatre, which we dedicate tonight to the better things of the drama—yes.

Our pageant tonight, dear friends, which is presented by the Girl Scouts of Potsville and directed by Mrs. Bessie Ketchum, Potsville's own elocution teacher, is entitled, "America, Where Art Thou?" Isn't that a sweet title? So intriguing!

Owing to a slight delay back stage, dear friends, I want to announce, before the pageant begins, the name of the winner of the prize winning poem, written in honor of this occasion. I know you are all anxiously awaiting the decision. Yes.

I want to say, first of all, that the judges had

a very, very difficult time in making the selection, for so many meritorious efforts were handed in. Yes. Particular mention should be given to the poem written by little Elsie Plunkett, the daughter of Judge and Mrs. Plunkett and, I might proudly add, my niece—yes—who is here with us tonight. Her poem is being published tonight in the POTSVILLE GAZETTE, which is edited by her father. Yes. It is entitled, "My City, 'Tis of Thee," and resembles, in a way, our national anthem. As I read it, I said to myself, "Is it possible that this remarkable child is only twelve years old? Why, she writes with all the deep penetration and power of a girl poet of fourteen!"

However, as children are admitted free anyway, it was decided to give the award, which consists of two seats for each of the six different pageants to be given here this summer, to Mrs. Alvira Chunk for her truly remarkable work of art, which she has very appropriately entitled, "Thou, Potsville."

May I read it to you, dear friends?

THOU, POTSVILLE

Thou, Potsville!
Oh, village beautiful!
An orchid to thee!

Thou, Potsville!
We, thy native sons,
Accept now thy challenge!

Isn't it thrilling?

Town of our birth,
Seat of our inspiration!
Thou, Potsville!

And to us, who were not born here,
City of our adoption.

I came among you at the age of eight.
If I had come a year earlier,
I should have been only seven.

Really an epic, isn't it?

You took an alien in
And made her one with you.

And here I want to add that Mrs. Chunk, as you perhaps know, really was an alien, having come here at the age of eight—seven—eight—from Greenville, which is twenty-six miles south of here.

And made her one with you.
Thou, Potsville!

"Full many a gem of poorest ray serene
The dark, unfathomed caves of ocean bare;
Full many a flower is born to blush unseen."
But not thou, Potsville!

I know we are all very proud, dear friends, to have such a truly remarkable poet in our midst.

And, now, if you will excuse me for just a second, I will see if they are ready to begin.

Are you ready to begin back there? No? Why, whatever is the matter? Well, we will have to go on without them. We can't wait any longer. Dear friends, owing to the non-appearance of four of the principals, who missed the bus from Centerville, we will omit the first act and begin with the second. If they arrive in time, we will go back and do the first act later.

Happy performance, dear, dear friends!

LITTLE ITALY

LITTLE ITALY

Come in. Yes, Mrs. Vaccaro. He's asleep at last, thank God. I count the minutes because then he does not feel the pain so great.

No, thank you. You are very kind but I cannot eat. All I can do is think. My baby dead—my husband blind—shot down in the street by gangsters! That is this hellhole we call *Little Italy!*

Who? A reporter? Oh, send him away! I don't want to see him.

Why do you force yourself in here? What do you want of me? Do you think I do not have troubles enough? My heart is breaking and you ask me for pictures and a story!

Please go. My husband is asleep at last—for the first time since it happened. We must not awaken him. He doesn't know about Rosa yet! He doesn't know yet! I don't know how we're going to tell him. The doctors say we must not tell him for two—three days—till they know he is out of danger. He keeps asking about Rosa and I have to go out of the room for awhile and act as if I were coming in to see how she is and then go back and tell him she is better and will get well. Little Rosa was the treasure of his heart and she was my doll.

Yes, you may see her. Here she is. My little cold, white baby! I used to wish she could stay a baby always. She was so tiny and sweet. Now she won't ever grow up. Now she'll always be little—so little—my poor baby!

How could God do this to her? It makes me think there is no God or He would not let this happen! But, while my husband lives, I have to try to trust. I do not dare give up. If I lose him, too, I will never pray again.

Tell your paper that these things happen because the Italians are not courageous enough to come out and tell what they know. Myself—I was born in this country. But I know my people. There will not be one person on this street who will tell! Mrs. Raggini was standing at the window, watching the children at play in the street. Her little boy was killed before her eyes. She tore her hair out for sorrow but she says she saw nothing. I wish to God I had seen that car! If I ever set my hands on the man who killed my little Rosa, I will cut him into pieces!

But my people will not talk. They are afraid. The murderers will come again and kill—killing our children at play in the streets—sending them back to us bleeding and torn. It is a shame upon America! In Italy my people could not earn enough to live and here our children are killed before our eyes! Yet what can we do while the gang war goes on? The children must play somewhere. The street is all we have.

Hush! It's Michael! He's awake!

Yes, Michael! I'm coming, dear. I've just been getting Rosa to sleep.

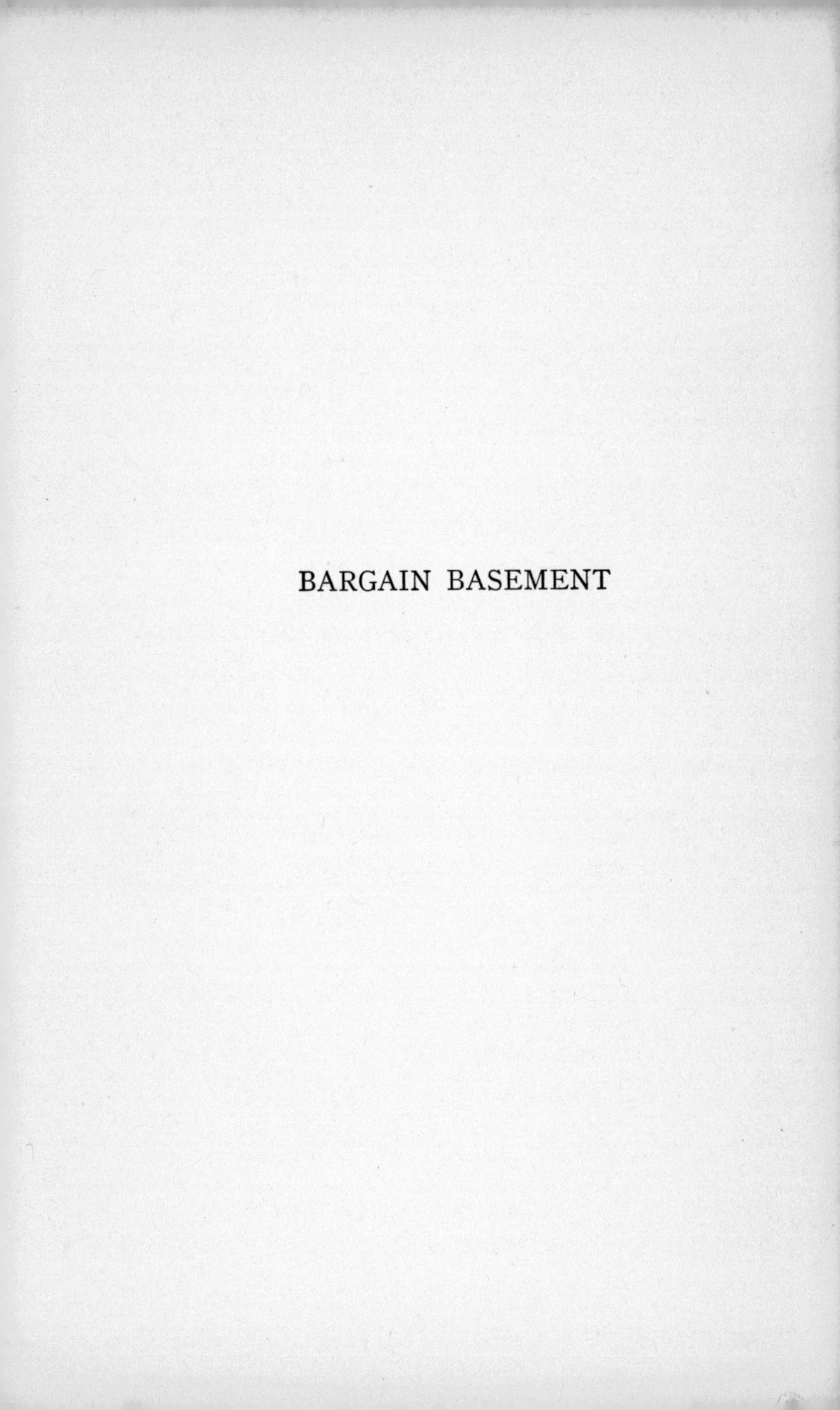

BARGAIN BASEMENT

BARGAIN BASEMENT

Say, Mayme! Come on over a minute if ya ain't busy! I got somethin' to tell ya.

Oh, it's about Fannie—funniest thing that ever happened around this store. Gee, it's a riot. Well, ya know, she's got a terrible case on that new floorwalker who wears the nose glasses —ya know—the one with the ribbon on 'em. Yeah, that's the one. She got transferred over to furniture polish just so she could be in his section, ya know. She told Mr. Murphy that she couldn't stand it here because the draft from the window was on her neck but the real reason was because she wanted to be over in his section. Gee, she can't fool me. Well, the second day she was over there, he comes up to her, see. I was over talkin' to Lily on my way back from the wrappin' desk—that's how I heard it. Of course, she don't know I know it, see. Well, as I was sayin', he comes up to her and she begins to smile all over when she sees him comin' and he says to her, he says, "Are ya doin' anything this evenin', Miss Greenberger?" he says, and she gets all *ex*cited and she answers him real hopeful like, ya know, and she says, "No, not a thing," she says, and he says, "Well, then, will ya try to be on time tomorrow mornin'?" he says. Gee, I like to died I laughed so hard. Of course, she don't know I know it, see. She has not the slightest particle of a idea that I know it and I'm not goin' to tell her, neither. Say, that one's too good to waste. But just wait till she gets fresh with me sometime. I'll let out on her right in front of everybody, I'll tell the world. Gee, I never will forget how *ex*cited she looked!

Oh, sure, I did. Gee, you ought to of. Swellest dance I've went to in over a year. Met the swellest fella. Gee, he's swell. Got eyes just like Clark Gable. And can he dance! Baby! I got a date with him Tuesday night. Gee, he's swell! I can't get over him. Drives a car and everything. Yeah. Truck for Wanamaker's.

Oh, I wore my new one. Didn't I tell ya I was goin' to? Yeah, I just got it out of the will call in time. Say, ya know, it's taken me so long to finish payin' for that dress it's all went out of style. I should worry, tho; I'm crazy about it anyway. It sure is becomin' to me and ya know it's all right really, because it goes way down to the floor in back, even if it is above the knees in front. It sure made a hit, too, I'll say! Ya know, this guy says to me I've got the best lookin' legs he's ever saw and he says it sure is like old times to see a girl's legs again, even if it's only in the front, and I says, "Well, I'm not goin' to pertend I haven't got any. My feet's got to be fastened to somethin'."

Excuse me, but this is my busy day.

Yes, moddom, we sells perculators. Third aisle to your left in the rear.

She wanted to know if we sells them. I suppose she thinks we gives 'em away.

Oh, there's the phone. Gee, as if I didn't have enough to contend with with the customers without the telephone ringin'.

Hello. Hardware speakin'. What? You have got the wrong party, moddom. I'm teakettles, clotheslines, flower pots and aluminum.

Gee, I hate to think of bein' in this department all my life. Did cha hear about Gertie? Ya didn't? Why, she got transferred up to gents' underwear, startin' this mornin'. Gee, that girl sure has got all the luck. I never seen the like of it. Ya know, I think I'll bleach my hair and see if I can get transferred up there. What would cha think about it? Yeah? I must say hers looks lovely. It sure is becomin' to her. Why, just plain peroxide, she told me. Yeah. She said she'd come over some night and help me do mine—just the first time, ya know. Her cousin helped her. She used to work in one of these beauty parlors before she got married and had so many kids.

Excuse me.

What, moddom? I'm sorry, moddom, but those are the sharpest tacks we've got.

Gee, this sellin' hardware sure is makin' me hard. I wish I could get a job in the underwear. Ya meet the swellest fellas in underwear—or else in the neckties.

Well, for cryin' out loud! Myrtle Bradley! Where did ju come from? Yeah? Gee, ya look *swell!* Where did ja get the baby? It's yours? Gee, ya sure work fast, don't chew?

Mayme, look who's here! Myrtle and she's got a baby, can ya beat it?

Gee, it sure is cute—lovely baby. I sure like babies a lot. My, she's the picture of health, ain't she? I mean, he certainly looks a lot like you—just the image. Ain't it the truth, Mayme? Don't cha think she looks just like Myrtle? Sure does, especially his eyes. Ain't it remarkable? My, what a big baby he is for his age—how old is she? Six months? Is that all? Well, what d'ya think of that? Pretty soon he'll be walkin' won't it?

Excuse me.

What is it, moddom? Fels Naptha soap? Counter 18 for soap, moddom.

Did cha get that? Gee, when she smiled her whole face went into an *e*clipse. Gee, I thought Valentines was all over but the Easter eggs are still runnin' around! She sure looks like nobody's business from the rear.

Say, where ya livin' now, Myrtle? New Rochelle? Gee, that's swell! Like it? Bet you're glad to be out of this dump, ain't cha? Say, didn't cha tell me your husband was a minister? Gee, that's swell. I don't suppose ya feel the depression so much in that field, do ya? Ya know, Flossie married a minister too. Yeah. She has been in to see me since. Well, personally, I think she done very well for herself. I sure do. Ya know, Flossie's no prize package.

Say, there's old Murphy eyein' us over there. Pertend like you're buyin' somethin', Myrtle. Oh, sure, he's still here. He'll never die. He's one of them darned immortals.

Excuse me.

What is it, moddom? That's extra strong

clothesline, moddom. Our special. 68¢, moddom.

I wish she'd buy it and go hang herself. Gee, that's the way it is all day long. You never seen the like of it.

Well, moddom, I'm givin' ya as little attention as possible. Well, that's what cha asked for, wasn't it—a little attention? Did cha want the clothesline? 68¢, moddom.

Cayash! Caayaash! Calling Caayaaash! Number 127!

Gee, I'll be 127 by the time she gets here. She's tyin' French knots in her chewin' gum and flirtin' with that new guy demonstratin' eggbeaters. She's over there all the time. Gee, what she sees in him is beyond me. Ya know, she says to me the other day, she says, "Gee, Ruby," she says, "have ya saw that guy makin' eyes at me?" And I says, "I have not noticed it." "Well, he does," she says, "all day long, even while he's demonstratin'." "Gee, dearie," I says, "can't cha do any better than that?" I says. "Oh," she says, "I know what's the matter with you. You're just jealous." "Jealous!" I says. "Say, I turn down guys that make him look sicker'n usual every day. Just because he's got a little *mus*tache," I says, "don't let that deceive ya none. It takes more'n a *mus*tache," I says, "to make a man and don't chew believe otherwise," I says. I certainly told it to her, I'll tell the world. . . . Goldie! Cayash!

Gee, ya shriek for cayash but ya never get any.

Excuse me just a moment, moddom. I'll get your change.

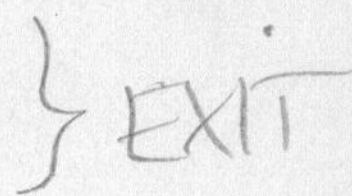

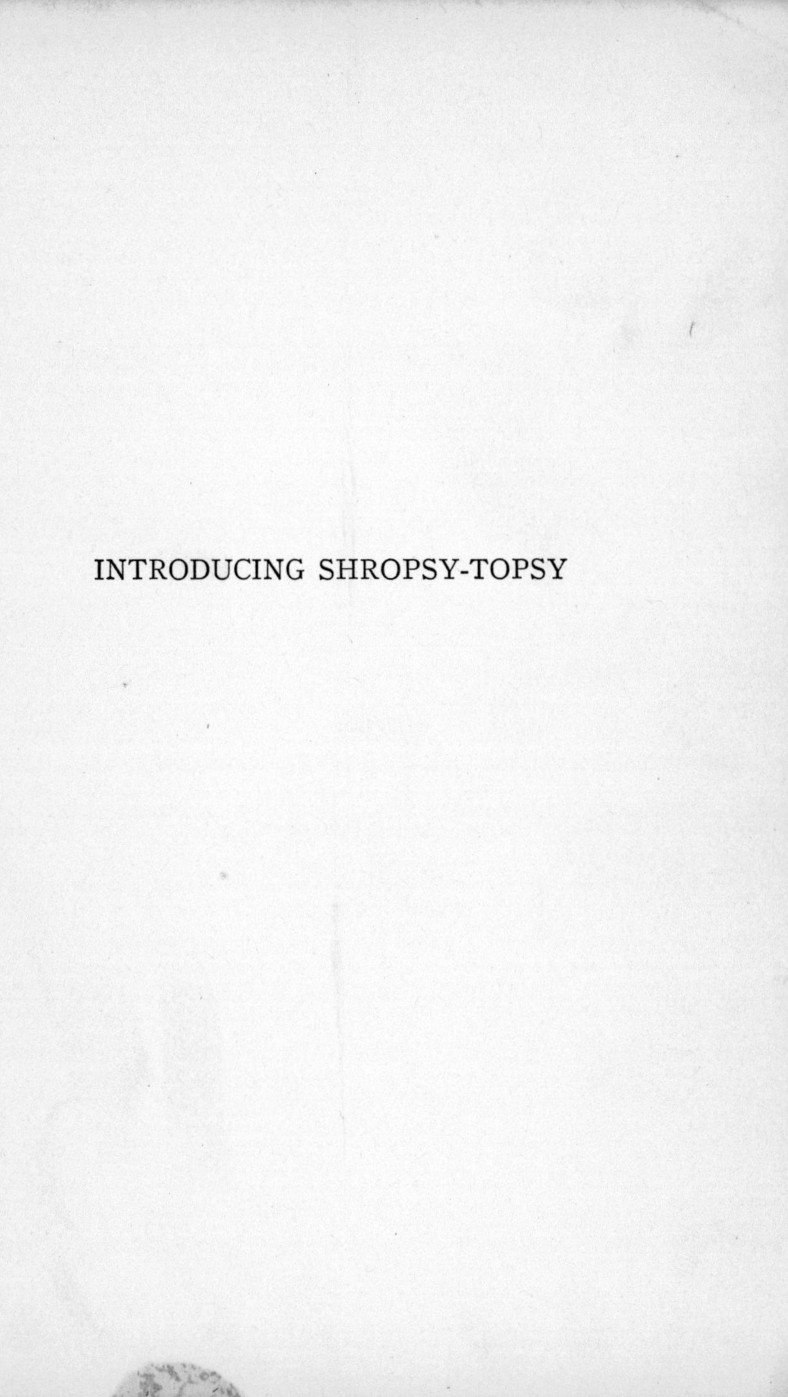

INTRODUCING SHROPSY-TOPSY

INTRODUCING SHROPSY-TOPSY

(A Department Store Rhapsody)

IntrodoocingShropsyTopsytheperfectfoodin thepinkpaaackage. Good for old and young—sick and well—everybody likes it. Step right up and get your free sample. FreesampleofShropsy Topsytheperfectfoodinthepinkpackage. Shrop—

Hello, Mr. Gilicuddy. Am I doin' all right? Well, of course, I have not really learned it yet. I can't say it as fast as I will be able to after I've had more practise. Oh, yeah, I sure do thank ya, Mr. Gilicuddy. I sure am glad to be out of that basement. Of course, I really only regard this as a steppin' stone to the underwear, ya know. That's where I want to get eventually—men's underwear. Ya meet the swellest fellas in underwear. My girl friend got transferred up there and she told me. But I always say one floor at a time and I sure am glad to be out of the basement. Yeah. O. K., I will see ya later. Goodbye, Mr. Gilicuddy.

IntrodoocingShropsyTopsytheperfectfoodin thepinkpaackage. Everybody likes it. Step right up and get your free sample.

Yes, moddom, it's free. No, moddom, they's no charge. Only one, moddom.

IntrodoocingShropsyTopsytheperfectfoodin thepinkpaackage.

Shropsy-Topsy, moddom? Free sample of Shropsy-Topsy. Yes, moddom, we gives it away. No, moddom, we don't sells it. Yes, moddom, we sells it but in the big packages. Only 25¢, moddom. 89¢ in the largest size—contains five times as much. It's cheaper in the big packages, moddom. Yes, moddom, you can have your free sample besides, moddom. Charge? Yes, moddom, give your charge to the girl at the side. Elsie, take a charge for moddom.

IntrodoocingShropsyTopsytheperfectfoodin thepinkpackage. Everybody likes it—old and young—women and children.

What, moddom? Is it like Wheatena? Is Kate Smith like Rudy Vallee?

ShropsyTopsytheperfectfoodinthepinkpaackage. Step right up and get your free sample. FreesampleofShropsyTop—

Oh, yes, moddom, they's full of vitaphones.

A and B? Why, moddom, they's way up to S. What, moddom? You don't believe they is an S? Oh, yes, they is, moddom. It's a new one they haven't discovered yet. We get 'em here before they even come out, moddom.

ShropsyTopsytheperfectfoodinthepinkpaackage. Step right up and get your free sample—free sample of ShropsyTop—

I said free *sample*—not *samples,* lady. You've been here four times already. Please, moddom. Please, moddom, Ladies, don't crowd. Please—one at a time. They's plenty of samples for everybody. No, little boy, we don't give samples to children. Yes, moddom, Shropsy-Topsy's good for children but we don't give samples to children. Please, moddom, don't grab like that. This ain't a help yourself cafeteria. That's what I'm here for. Yes, moddom, we gives 'em away but by the package—not the carload.

ShropsyTopsytheper—

What, moddom? Grapenuts? No, moddom, not here. At the grocery counter behind the brassieres. Well, why don't the Fords sell Chevrolets, moddom? It's the same principle. This is a special Shropsy-Topsy counter. We don't sell Grapenuts.

ShropsyTopsytheperfectfood. ShropsyTop—

Hello, Agnes. Well, it's better than the basement anyway.

ShropsyTopsytheper—

What, Agnes? Tonight? No, I ain't got one.

ShropsyTop—

What, Agnes? Oh, gee, that would be swell. Are ya sure ya can fix it? Who with?

ShropsyTop—

The guy in the blue shirt? Gee, that would be swell. You know, as a rule, I do not like blind dates but I sure would like to be with him on one. Gee, that would be swell!

ShropsyTop—

8:30? Gee, thanks a lot, Agnes.

ShropsyTop—

What, Agnes? O. K., Agnes. 8:30 in front of the *Ho*tel Astor. O. K., Agnes, I will be there.

ShropsyTopsytheper—

What, moddom? All the way to the rear, moddom. You'll see the sign. The little boy will have to go to the other side.

ShropsyTop—

Elsie, what time is it? Twelve o'clock? Thank heavens! You take the counter. I'm going to *lunch!*

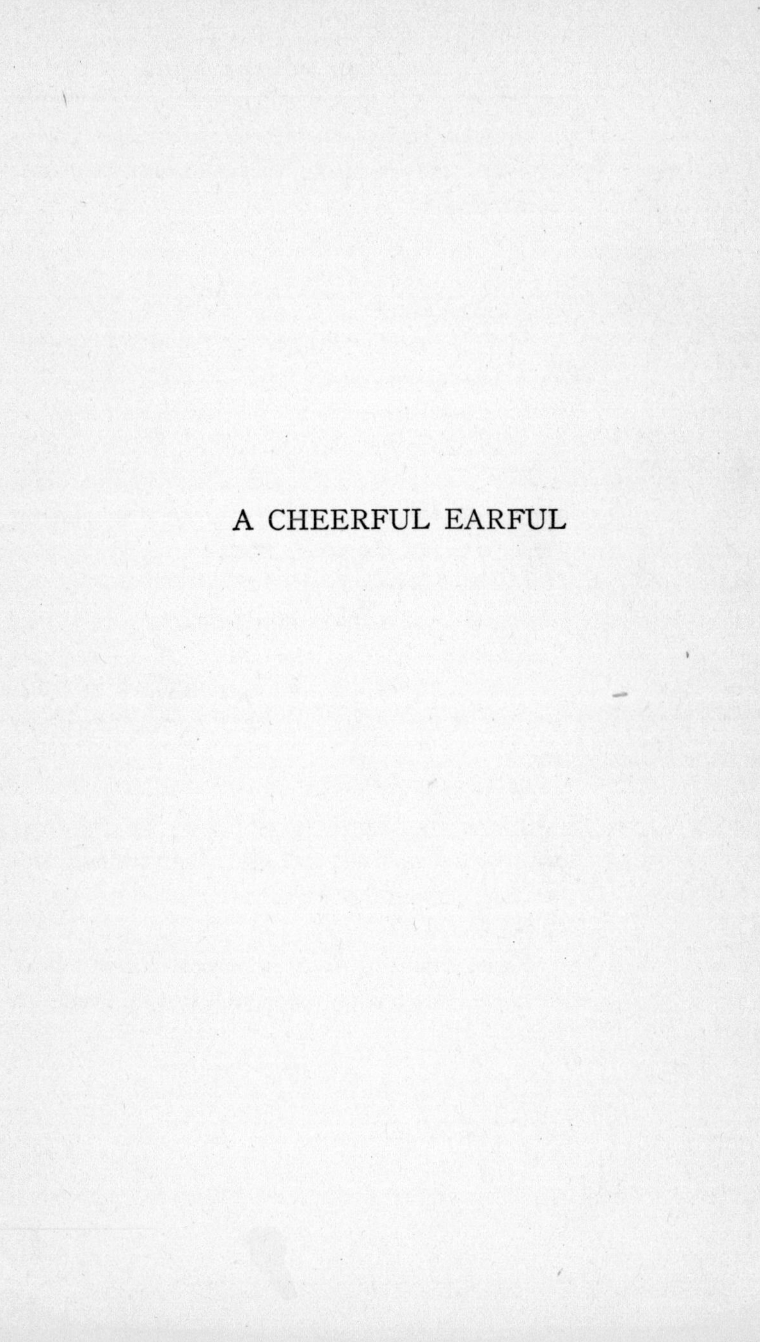

A CHEERFUL EARFUL

A CHEERFUL EARFUL

Acknowledgment for the basis of this sketch is made to Mary Kyle Dallas. It is included in this book because it has so long been identified with Miss Moffett's performances.

Yes. Well, I'll bring them piny plants up to-morrow. Yes. All right. Good-bye.

Well, how do you do, Curnelia? I heerd you wuz sick, so I thought I'd drop in and cheer you up a little. Besides, I said to myself, as I come up the stairs, "This may be the last time I ever see Curnelia Jane alive."

What's that? You ain't goin' to die yit? Well, how do you know you ain't? There wuz poor Mis' Jones. She wuz asettin' up and everybody wuz asayin' how smart she wuz and all of a sudden she wuz tuk with a spasm and went off like a flash. Yes. Oh, my, it wuz turrible.

I brung you what wuz left of the medicine she tuk. It never done her no good but you might like to try it. It's probly a sight bettern that stuff you're takin'. It's plain that ain't helpin' you none. Oh, no, you ain't really feelin' good,

Curnelia. You're just sayin' that. Why, ya look turrible.

Of course, the main thing to do now is jest keep caam—don't fret yourself. Of course, things can't go on jest as if you wuz downstairs. You can't expect that. I wonder if you knew your little Billy wuz asailin' around in a tub on the mill pond. Yes. And your little Sammy. Your little Sammy wuz alettin' your little Jimmy down in the well in a clothes basket.

My land, what's the matter? Well, I guess Providence will take keer of them, seein' there ain't nobudy else to. What say? Ya thought Bridget wuz? Well, you thought wrong. She ain't. I seen her down to the back gate as I come in, atalkin' to a strange man. Yes. He looked to me like a burglar. Oh, I 'spect she give him the imprint of the door key in wax and he'll come in tonight and murder you all. There wuz that family up on Kobble Hill wuz murdered last week for fifty dollars. Yes—the hull family.

Now, don't fidget so. It will be bad for the bebby. Let me see him. Poor little dear. How singular it is, to be sure, you never can tell at that age whether a child's deef or dumb or blind or crippled or an idiot. It might be all of 'em and you'd never know it. Most of them that does have their senses, tho, make bad use of 'em. That ought to be your comfort if anything should be the matter with him. Then, too, lots of 'em don't live more'n a year. I seen a bebby's funeral as I come up the block.

Well, ya got some tube roses, ain't ya, Curnelia? I thought I smelled 'em, even with my cold. Tube roses allus makes me think of funerals. We had so many of 'em in the house when Milly died.

How's Mr. Kobble? Finds it warm in town, eh? Well, I'd think he would. My land, they're droppin' down by hundreds with sunstroke in the city. Then, if it ain't sunstroke, it's them turrible trains he rides on twice a day. It's just triflin' with death. Oh, dear me, all the turrible things that hang over us all the time—it's—it's turrible.

Scarlet fever's broke out down in the village, Curnelia. Yes. Little Isaac Potter's got it. Yes. I seen your little Jimmy playin' with him last Saturday.

Well, I got to be gittin' along. I got another sick friend I got to cheer up. I never feel I've done my duty unless I see 'em all before I sleep. Well, good-bye, Curnelia. My land, you look so pale, Curnelia. I don't think you got a very good doctor. I wish you'd send him away and git another one. Why, you don't look so good as you did when I come in.

Well, I got to be gittin' along. If the worst comes to the worst, let me know and I'll come in and cheer you up, if I can't do anything else. Well, good-bye, Curnelia. Good-bye. Good-bye.

AN ENGLISH LADY'S IMPRESSIONS OF AMERICA

AN ENGLISH LADY'S IMPRESSIONS OF AMERICA

How do you do, Lady Teasdale? I'm SO glad to see you. My, what a lot of people have turned out! I shall be quite panic stricken addressing them all!

How do you do, Mrs. Chittendon? This is a pleasure. Yes, isn't there a crowd? I didn't expect so many.

Nancy, darling! How perfectly sweet to see you again! I was SO hoping you would be here. Oh, I've only been back a week, you know, and they told me you were in the country, which is why I didn't phone. Oh, I'm splendid, thank you, darling. I'm SO happy to be home again. Well, there's no place like England, is there?

Oh, we had a delightful crossing. I stayed in bed all the time we were out—enjoyed myself thoroughly. Well, I wasn't taking any chances. Going over it was just TOO terrible. Darling, don't ask me about it. I *couldn't* tell you.

How do you do, my dear Bishop Chudleigh?

I'm SO happy to see you again. And how is your gout today? I said, HOW IS YOUR GOUT TODAY? Oh, I'm SO glad. Yes, isn't there a crowd? I'm quite terrified, I assure you. Yes, I think that's an excellent idea. Yes, I think so—just a short prayer and your address of welcome. Yes, I'm quite ready, thank you—as ready as I ever will be. I'll sit right here, where I'll be quite accessible. Then you can just nod when you're ready.

(BUSINESS)

Ladies of the committee—dear Bishop Chudleigh—ladies.

I want to thank Bishop Chudleigh for his very gracious words of introduction and all of you for the very warm reception you have accorded me this afternoon.

It is with the greatest pleasure that I stand before you today. As you know, I have just returned from my long journey to America. Bishop Chudleigh and our dear Lady Teasdale have asked me to speak to you this afternoon, regarding my impressions of America.

My trip was in the nature of a lecture tour—to aid in bringing closer together the two great English speaking countries in the great work we have undertaken in the cause of the Christian colonization of India. By Christian, I mean, of course, Episcopalian.

To begin with, America is quite large. In fact, I might almost say it is VERY large. I didn't have an opportunity to see all of it, so I can only give you a very general idea.

The nicest people, I understand, live in the vicinity of Boston. I met several very charming ladies there and they told me that the nicest people come from there. It is a very charming place.

They have a most peculiar custom, however. Wherever there has been a serious accident, they erect some sort of monument. They have a very elaborate one in particular, I remember, at some place there—I think they call it Bunker Hill. I believe they told me a man named Warren or Warner or some such name fell there. It must have been a nasty fall. I think it killed him. Anyway, they have a monument erected there—a very steep one—to sort of commemorate the fall, I expect.

The Americans are exceedingly keen people. They seem to have a way of finding out everything about you without your knowing it. It gives you a most uncomfortable feeling sometimes. I know, one afternoon I was motoring along the highway and I came to a sign, which read, "Drive slow. This means YOU." It was most disconcerting, I must say. It gave me a most peculiar feeling and, you know, I haven't been able to figure out yet how they knew I was there. Of course, I suppose they got it from the passport but, even so, I don't see why they should feel it necessary to warn me about it, for I have never been what you would call a rapid driver.

The American women are exceedingly good looking—very much alive and all that sort of thing. One could almost call them beautiful except that they wear the MOST atrocious clothes—particularly hats. I don't know where they ever get them. It doesn't seem to be so much a question of economy, for they seem to spend an appalling amount of money on clothes. I think that it's just that they need someone to go with them and tell them what's becoming.

What is it, Bishop? Louder? Louder.

The American men are exceedingly gallant—by far the most gallant of any I have ever met anywhere. I had a most vivid example of that going over. It was so dreadfully rough and practically everyone on board was seasick; at least, that's the reason they gave for not giving us a particle of attention. Well, the MOST awful thing happened—you can't imagine. I was so terribly ill and I rang and rang but no one answered. Finally, I slipped a wrapper on over my nightgown—I was much too ill to think about dressing—and managed to stagger over to the adjoining stateroom to ask for assistance; I thought if I could just get some bicarbonate of soda or something, you know, it might relieve me. Well, I knocked and some sort of a voice told me to come in, which I did, and found, to my horror, that there was a man in bed. He was evidently as ill as I. Now, wouldn't you have thought that the authorities might have foreseen some such predicament and arranged to have a woman next to me? I thought it MOST peculiar. Of course, I was frightfully embarrassed and emitted a faint scream, which was all I could muster in my condition. It was terribly mortifying—very compromising. But he was most gallant, I must say, and he said VERY soothingly, "Don't worry, my dear lady; it's quite all right. I'll never live to remember," which I thought was VERY considerate of him. I must say I've never met an Englishman so considerate.

Well, coming back I didn't take any chances.

I just went to bed and stayed there the entire time we were out. Everyone said it was just imagination but I said, "Imagination, indeed! I was never sick before in my life except once and that was two years ago when I had indigestion."

Another very peculiar characteristic of the American people is that of extreme secrecy. This is especially true in certain localities. If you thank them for any reason, they are very apt to say, "Don't mention it," which struck me as being most peculiar, for, in the majority of cases, what had transpired was not a tall of a confidential nature. Altho I recognized it as a serious breach of etiquette, I accepted it, for some time, as merely an idiosyncrasy of the people and, unlike most English people, refrained from telling them that, in England, it was never necessary to ask a well bred person not to repeat a conversation.

One time, tho, I must confess, I became quite irritated by it. I was stopping at a hotel in—what was the name of that town—one of those queer names they have in America—Elephant, I believe it was—no, that wasn't it. Just a moment while I consult my notes. Oh, yes, yes . . . Buffalo . . . that was it . . . Buffalo. I was stopping at a hotel there—one that seemed perfectly respectable—a trifle garish, perhaps, but, nevertheless, respectable. I was lecturing that evening before quite a large gathering and wished to rest after my journey, so I left instructions at the desk that I was not to be disturbed unless a certain gentleman, who was in charge of the meeting, called to see me. The clerk said that he would see that my wishes were carried out. I thanked him, as a matter of course, to which he said, "Don't mention it, madam." Well, I thought that was going a bit too far, so I turned upon him and I said, "See here, young man. There is no occasion for any such remark. The gentleman in question is calling upon me for strictly business purposes. As a matter of fact," I said, "he happens to be related to a distant branch of my family and, if I receive him in my sitting room, you may rest assured that all the proprieties will be observed. My work," I said, "is among diligent and religious female orphans and my character, I assure you, is quite above reproach. Moreover," I added, "if this is the type hotel which countenances loose conduct, it is well that I have learned it before I have stayed the night." And I left, in spite of his remonstrances and apologies, to which I steadfastly refused to listen. At a time like that, it is well to show character with a firm hand.

Another little incident which occurred while I was in America emphasizes the truth of my contention that Englishwomen, with their perfect poise and unruffled tempers, prove themselves mistresses of any occasion.

I was walking in the country one morning and had my arms full of some very lovely autumn leaves I had gathered. You can imagine my astonishment, not to say consternation, when, farther down the road, I was accosted by a most uncouth man, who was working in a nearby field and who came running toward me, waving his arms in a most alarming manner and shouting excitedly, at the top of his voice, "Hey, lady! Drop that poison ivy!" Well, for a moment, I admit, I was startled by such conduct but I quickly recovered, very calmly drew myself up to my full height, looked him straight in the eye and said, "Tut! Tut! Calm yourself, my good man. This wasn't picked on your land." He gave me a most peculiar look. I think he was rather overcome for a moment. Then he simply turned and walked away, without saying another word.

I quote this little incident because it points out so vividly the truth of my contention that even a laborer of the lower classes is instinctively conscious of mental, as well as social, superiority.

America is still quite wild, I believe, in spots, altho I didn't see that section of it. They evidently have large quantities of wild animals in the cities, however, of which they must take exceedingly good care. I passed one quite large white building—entirely white, I remember—on which it said in very ornate, gold letters, "Eagle Dry Cleaners." Of course, the eagle is the American national bird and I presume they give it more particular care than they do some of the other animals. I thought it quite remarkable, tho.

Altho America is, as we all know, a democracy, they evidently have some peculiar system of royalty. I must admit I don't understand just how it is managed. It doesn't seem to be so much a question of national government but certain individuals and organizations apparently have some such power. I met one gentleman at a luncheon, who was, I believe he said, the president of the local Rotary Circle. We were discussing food, I remember, and I remarked that many very famous cooks were decorated abroad—particularly in France—to which he replied quite casually that he often felt like crowning his. Something happened at that moment, so I didn't have an opportunity to go into it with him. I presume, however, that, being the president of the Rotary Circle, which is evidently a branch or some sort of an offspring of the Knights of the Round Table, he had that power. I thought it was MOST interesting.

Well, now I feel that I have taken up more than my share of time. There are any number of other things which I could tell you about America but time does not permit.

May I thank you all very much for your very kind attention?

Bishop Chudleigh, do you think they could hear me in the rear? My voice usually carries like a bell but I had a severe attack of laryngitis while in America, from which I have never completely recovered. Oh, I don't know what I shall do if my voice goes. It's SO important to me in my work.

Oh, I think perhaps that would help. Punch IS a great strengthener of the voice, I am told. How VERY thoughtful of you to suggest it. Yes, let us go and have some, by all means.

Yes, Lady Teasdale, I'll be back in a moment. The dear Bishop suggests that I have just a drop of punch. It clears the voice so beautifully. Yes, we'll be back in a moment—in plenty of time for the music. Yes. Yes, I only want a drop!

A PHILADELPHIA MOTHER VISITS SCHOOL

A PHILADELPHIA MOTHER VISITS SCHOOL

Junior, take your fingers out of your mouth, dorling. Remember what a big boy you are. You're almost as big as the children going to school. Come along like a little man, now, and say, "How do you do?" to the teacher.

Good-morning, Miss Chester. I thought Junior and I would visit school this morning.

Say, "How do you do?" to Miss Chester, Junior. Take your fingers out of your mouth, dear.

Oh, Miss Chester, we're just so anxious to see how Annabelle is getting along!

What, dear? Where is she? Well, now let's see if we can find her. See which one can find her first. There she is—over in the corner! See?

Hello, dorling!

This is the first time we've ever seen our Annabelle in school, isn't it, Junior?

Oh, thank you, Miss Chester.

Sit up here by mother, Junior.

You know, Miss Chester, I used to go quite often last year when she had Miss Bloomer. Miss Bloomer used to say to me, "Mrs. Stanwyck," she said, "Annabelle isn't like other children. It isn't only that she's brighter than they are but there's just something different about her, that's all."

Take your fingers out of your mouth, Junior.

I beg your pordon? Yes, I know; most of the children in her class are three or four years younger than she is but both Mr. Stanwyck and I would rather have it that way. We've always said we'd rather have her strong and healthy and not try to make her strain her mind. I think that's dangerous, don't you? We don't want to push her, you know, especially as she's so precocious.

Of course, there's one thing I *never* do and that's talk about my children but you're her teacher, so I know you understand. It's the most morvelous thing the way she can imitate people. Haven't you noticed it? You haven't? Well, you ought to see her take off our cook—it's just killing!

Oh, Annabelle! Annabelle, come up here, dorling. I want you to do Ella for Miss Chester, dear. She's never seen you do it. Now, stand off there and do it nicely, dear. Just as she comes thru the doorway. Now, don't act so silly, dorling. That isn't funny. Because mother says it isn't. Mother knows what's funny and that isn't funny! Now stand off there and do it nicely, dorling.

Isn't that *killing?* She just keeps us roaring all the time. Of course, everyone has always said that I should have gone on the stage myself and I suppose she—

What did you say? Yes, she does cry easily. She's so sensitive. Not many people understand a nature like hers. I'm so glad that you do.

Take your fingers out of your mouth, Junior.

I don't know what makes him do that, Miss Chester. I'm sure I don't.

Here, blow, dorling. *Blow.* Blow *hord.* That's better.

Oh, yes, he is big for his age. And strong! You can't imagine. But I'm so porticular about the children's food. They have everything in just the proper proportions. I never have any difficulty except with spinach. I don't know how he comes by it. All my family were very fond of spinach and Albert's people are *great* spinach eaters but Junior won't even touch it. Now with Annabelle it's carrots. I have to slice them and tell her it's cheese. But Junior loves carrots. I never have a bit of trouble about them with him. Yes, I suppose that's why he is so strong. Do you know he walked and talked before he was a year old? Well, he gets it right from my people. My mother often used to say that, when I was a year old, I had all the ways of a child of two. And Junior takes right after me. Why, you know, even now, he notices every street car and cries if he can't have it. You know, my younger brother *studied* engineering before he went in the furniture business and I shouldn't be at all surprised if that wasn't where he got it.

What's that? The bell? Why, it isn't time for the children to go home yet, is it? It *is?*

Well, get your coat, Annabelle, dorling. Hurry. Mother has things to do.

But I've always said, Miss Chester, it is a poor mother who can't spare the time to inquire how her children are getting along. I'm so glad that Annabelle is doing so well.

What, dorling? What? Well, we're going home right away now.

Well, you did hurry, didn't you, Annabelle? Say good-bye to Miss Chester now, dear.

Throw her a kiss, Junior.

Isn't that sweet? Oh, I do wish you could see

him having his breakfast! It's too cunning to see him trying to get the spoon in his mouth. I tell you—just come in any morning about twenty minutes after eight and then you can see it. Well, good-bye, Miss Chester. I'm so glad to hear just how Annabelle is doing. Good-bye. Good-bye.

Come along, dorlings. Come along.

Take your fingers out of your mouth, Junior!

A DEBUTANTE AT A COUNTRY CLUB DANCE

A DEBUTANTE AT A COUNTRY CLUB DANCE

Oh, isn't it just too divine out here! What a heavenly night! Of course, I just adore dancing and it really is the most divine party I was ever at in my life but I never felt such an irresistible desire to escape—to get out in the air where I could really breathe! Didn't you feel the same way? Exactly! That's the marvelous part about it! We both thought the same thing at absolutely the identical moment! I think it's the most amazing thing! Right in the middle of that heavenly waltz, suddenly I stopped, I remember—do you remember when I stopped?—and I thought, "I simply must get out and away or I shall stifle." And you just seemed to read my thoughts and simply steered me to the door. It was the most amazing thing!

Shall we sit down? Let's!

Oh! I think it's too divine! What a heavenly night! Oh, I could just drive and drive and never come back! Shall we? Oh, I'd adore it! How in the world did you guess that that's the one thing I wanted to do? Oh, you're too marvelous! But I think we'd better wait for a few more dances, don't you? Then I can just sort of get my wrap and we can sort of slip away without being missed.

Do you really? Oh, I think that's too marvelous. You know, you're the only man I know to whom I can really talk about anything serious. I'll never forget how you impressed me the first time I ever met you. Why, I certainly do. I remember it perfectly. I certainly do. We were being awfully silly about something or other, I remember, and then, suddenly, we got frightfully serious and began talking about all sorts of things!

Were you really? Well, that's awfully sweet of you to say so. You know, altho I've never seen you more than three times, I feel as tho I'd known you all my life! I know that sounds trite but I really do.

Do you really? Oh, I think it's the most marvelous thing the way you understand. So few men do, you know. They think a girl only wants to dance and flirt and run around like mad constantly. I know I never stop one minute. I dance my legs off. I just race around twenty-four hours of the day practically and, when it's all over, I think, "Where am I? What does it all mean anyway?" I know. Absolutely. That's my point exactly. It's all very well to race around and have a good time but there are times when you want to get away where it's perfectly quiet and get frightfully serious and talk about things that are really fundamental. I know. Absolutely. That's my point exactly.

I know all my friends say, "Gertrude, you're so frightfully serious at times." And I say, "Well, I can't help it. I was born with brains and I've got to use them!"

I know. Why, I know when I'm not doing anything else, I'm reading. I'm just reading all the time if I haven't anything else to do. And, if I'm not doing that, I'm seeing plays. I think that's so educational, don't you? I mean, so few people seem to go with that idea in mind. Or perhaps—well, I don't know. Don't you think so? I mean, do you really?

Oh, I saw the most marvelous play the other night. I can't think of the name of it. Did you see it? Well, it's all about crime or vice or something like that—too thrilling! No, that isn't it. I don't think that's it. It was a longer name, if you know what I mean, and it begins with M or something like that and it rhymes with something else, if you know what I mean.

Well, I'll think of it in a minute. It really isn't surprising I can't think of it this minute, for I have my mind so full of this new book I'm reading that I can't think of another thing. That's the way I am. I absorb everything so completely that, while I'm reading something, like a book, other things simply don't exist. They simply don't *exist!*

And this one is really the most divine book I ever read. Honestly, it's a scream! It really impressed me frightfully. Well, I can never think of his name—that awfully funny person who writes things. Well, let's see. It's some awfully funny title. Funny, I can't for the life of me think of it this minute but it's really terribly amusing. What's it about? Well, it's really terribly amusing—you know—one of those sort of fundamental things. I think his books are wonderful anyway, don't you? Why, this man whose name I can never think of, I mean.

Did you really? Oh, isn't that intriguing? Oh, how pricelessly perfect! Oh, I think that's absolutely divine! I know. Absolutely! Exactly, isn't it poisonous?

You know, that's the absolutely marvelous

part about you. You're so understanding. I mean, you actually are. So few men realize that a girl wants to get frightfully serious. They think that she just wants to hear them say how beautiful she is. I know. Absolutely. That's my point exactly. I abhor having men tell me I'm beautiful. I mean, I actually do and that's all I hear and I simply abhor it, because I mean I'd much rather have a man admire me for my character and my brains, because I mean it's really nothing to be beautiful. Do you think it is?

I know and I mean I think it's perfectly ridiculous for girls to want men to keep telling them they're beautiful. I mean I think it's perfectly absurd because I mean they must realize a man is just giving them a line, unless a girl's awfully dumb or something.

I know. I know I'm the only girl I know of who'd rather have a man admire her for her brains than her looks. That's what none of the men seem to realize and that's why I've been simply dying to get away and have a frightfully serious talk about things that are really fundamental.

Oh, do you really think I have? I know but I don't think most men—not you, of course, but most men—like a girl to have sense unless she's beautiful, do you? Well, I suppose it is important, isn't it?

Oh, it must be heavenly to be really beautiful! I don't mean just plain pretty but really beautiful!

What do you mean, I ought to know? Honestly, my dear, I never heard anything so completely puzzling as a remark like that! How in the world should I know? Why the idea! I'm not a tall! Do you honestly think I am? Well, I don't think I am a tall but it's awfully sweet of you to say so! Do you really think I am? Well, I'm positively thrilled that you think so! I mean, I actually am!

Let's go for that drive now, shall we? I don't think I'll need my wrap after all!

VERA CHEERA'S MORNING SUNSHINE TALK

VERA CHEERA'S MORNING SUNSHINE TALK

Good-morning, Mr. Cuddleby! Good-morning, Mr. Control Man! Isn't this a lovely morning?

What? Late? Oh, my sakes, am I? My sakes, it must have been the rain held up the traffic. Well, I'm already to begin.

Good-morning, dear unseen audience everywhere! This is Vera Cheera coming to you with her morning sunshine talk. . . . Just a minute, dear audience. Mr. Cuddleby has something to say. What is it, Mr. Cuddleby? We aren't on the air yet? Oh, that's what's the matter! I always feel so much more at home when the current is actually on. Yes. . . . .

Good-morning, dear, unseen audience everywhere! Just everywhere! This is Vera Cheera coming to you with her morning sunshine talk, thru the courtesy of Plunkett's Pink Pills for Pale People, bringing you a digest of the daily news, notes of cheer, beauty hints and hot weather recipes—not forgetting our little feathered friends!

First of all, radio friends, I want to say two special good-mornings this morning. One is to Mrs. Theophilus Gunter of Whirling Rapids, Texas, to tell her that her list of 7482 words, which she made out of the slogan, "Plunkett's Pink Pills for Pale People," has won the prize for the week of a free box of Plunkett's Pills.

I hope you will all enter this absorbing contest each week. It is absolutely free to everyone. All you have to do is to buy fifteen boxes of Plunkett's Pale Pills for Pink Peo—I beg your pardon—Plunkett's Pink Pills for Pink Peo—ah—Plunkett's *Pills*—tear off the top of each box and mail them, together with your list, to the contest editor, in care of this station. The person who sends in the longest correct list, together with the tops of the fifteen boxes, receives a free box of Plunkett's Pills absolutely free. Now isn't that an absorbing contest?

And I have a special summer suggestion for you, radio friends. Why not give a Plunkett's Pink Pills party and have each of your guests enter the contest? All you have to do is to buy fifteen boxes of Plunkett's Pills for each of your guests—have them tear off the top of the boxes themselves—it's more fun that way—and mail them, together with their separate lists—to the contest editor. Isn't that a lovely idea? And I have another big surprise for you, radio friends. The makers of Plunkett's Pills will send a special entry blank for each of your guests, if you will just write to me—Vera Cheera—in care of this station and tell me how many will be at your party! Isn't that lovely?

And my other special good-morning this morning, radio friends, is for Mrs. Eliza Twitchell of Pittsburgh, who wins honorable mention with her list of 6983 words. Better luck next time, Mrs. Twitchell! Just buy fifteen more boxes of Plunkett's Pills and enter the contest next week and you may win the free box of Plunkett's Pills!

Well, now, let's start right in on the news for the day. I have the paper right here before me and I'll just skim over the headlines and see what's what . . . Let's see, now . . . "FRANCE PAYS WAR DEBT IN FULL . . . HITLER ASSASSINATED IN GERMANY . . . STOCK MARKET GOES UP FORTY POINTS IN BRISK TRADING."

Well, there doesn't seem to *be* any news of importance this morning, radio friends, so we'll just go right on. Maybe something will happen before night and then Mr. Thomas and Mr. Hill can tell you about it.

So, now we come to our little health talk for the day, radio friends. Are you in a run down condition? Are you hard of hearing? Do you suffer from chills, fever, rheumatism, nerves, eczema, liver trouble, fallen arches, perspiration, appendicitis, eye strain, dental defects, heart trouble, apoplexy, constipation, bunions, false teeth, under nutrition, over nutrition, indigestion, insomnia, sleeplessness, halitosis, overweight, underweight, pink tooth brush or any of the other insidious things of which you are so apt to tell even your most casual acquaintances? Do not despair, radio friends. Relief is waiting for you! Just buy a box of Plunkett's Pink Pills for Pale People—or, better yet, buy fifteen boxes and enter our contest. You'll be amazed at the results. That tired feeling will vanish after you have taken your first Plunkett Pill!

Now, for the recipe for the day. Get out your pads and pencils, radio friends. I want to stress particularly the necessity of living on a simple diet during these hot, sultry days and this morning I have a special dessert for those friends of ours who are on a reducing diet. It is banana fudge cake, radio friends, and I recommend it to you particularly.

Take one large white layer cake—one large white layer cake—six ripe bananas—have you got that?—six ripe bananas—two pints of fudge sauce. I haven't time to give you the ingredients now but, if you will write to me, I will send you a typewritten copy telling just how to make it—two pints of fudge sauce. Slice the bananas—put between the layers—cover well with the fudge sauce and serve. I will repeat that. Slice the bananas. Put between the layers. Cover well with the fudge sauce and serve. Such a simple recipe and so good for you.

Now for the beauty hints for the day, dear audience, I want to talk to you, radio friends, about your elbows. You know, no matter how beautiful your face is, your appearance can be completely ruined by red, unsightly elbows. Therefore, radio friends, I have this encouragement to hold out to you. Crush three Plunkett Pills and mix them with your favorite cold cream. Rub this into your elbows before going to bed and you will be surprised how many of the pills you can use up that way!

And, now, radio friends, I bring you a wee, humble message about our little feathered friends. You know, birds sometimes need medical attention also, so I should advise you, radio friends, if you see a little sparrow drooping on your window sill, just crush some Plunkett's Pink Pills up and mix them with some bird seed and put it out for the birds. I will repeat that. Just crush up some Plunkett's Pink Pills. Mix them with some bird seed and put the mixture out for the birds. It is very simple.

And now the orchestra is going to play the William Tell overture. So, we're off, radio friends, to the steep mountain sides! I'm sure you'll all be wafted away on the wings of music to the Swiss mountains. So, until tomorrow at this same time, *bon voyage,* dear, unseen audience everywhere!

L'ESPIONNE

(*The Spy*)

L'ESPIONNE

(*The Spy*)

While the story itself is not authentic, part of the incidents in this sketch are based on the life of the famous Mata-Hari, greatest and most dangerous woman spy in all history.

The scene is a German court-martial during the World War.

You may take off the handcuff now. I will not run away.

Good-morning.

Thank you. I will stand.

My name? Why? Do you not know it? But why should I be arrested and brought before this court if you do not even know my name? Very well. For the sake of formality, I conform. My name, as you well know, is Maria de Castro, known on the stage as Jannine Dubois, a dancer. I am a subject of Spain and a member of your espionage service.

My age? That is also written on the record which you hold in your hand. As you can see,

I am young—or young enough. That is all that matters.

Treason is a strong word, General. You will find it hard to prove.

I will tell you. I was dancing in Paris at the outbreak of the war. Directly after, I came to Berlin to fill an engagement, the contract for which I had signed previously. The chief of police came to inspect my dancing costume, which had been reported insufficient. An intimacy developed between us. He was, I must confess, very indiscreet. He told me many secrets of war and then urged my admittance into the German secret service. In fact, to be quite truthful, he did more than urge it. He told me that, since he had been imprudent enough to acquaint me with the practices of this division, he must force me to become a member. If I refused . . . I did not refuse. I had already signed a contract for that fall to go again to Paris. This enabled me to cross the frontier without suspicion. I returned in the employ of the German secret service. The rest you know.

But I did not do so under protest. You are quite mistaken. Herr von Gruttsmacher's urging was not necessary. I was more happy than you know to join.

That is quite true. I was in constant touch with the French espionage service. Of course. The chief of that division was my lover. How else was I to obtain the information which was so necessary to you? Do you think I could have secured it from the streets?

That is also quite true. I did receive money from him. I admit it. But it was not the salary of a spy, as you accuse, but the price of my favors. I was his mistress—in your behalf.

After all, you forget. I am neither French nor German and I am in your employ. Is this the way you repay your spies?

False or otherwise, they were sent thru no fault of mine. Am I to be blamed because my messages were intercepted and the code changed? I was watched, I tell you.

That is not correct. And it proves nothing.

Very well, then. I will tell you, since you are determined to know. I have tried to keep silent but you make it impossible. The chief of this division, as I told you, lured me into your service. He was my lover. Since my return, I have avoided him and he is jealous. He is using this means to force me to his will. Can he deny it?

That is utterly grotesque. It is false from beginning to end. Because the information I sent to you from Paris proved to be incorrect, thru no mistake of mine, you really think that you have proved your case. You are incredible. You even surpass yourself.

He is irritated at me. I have been foolish enough to annoy him and he has invented this impossible story to revenge himself. Look at him now, if you do not believe me. He is mad with jealousy. He would sell his soul and his country just to be with me once again.

Malice! It's the last of your passions and, to satisfy it, you are willing to turn me over to a firing squad.

General! Do you really believe such a ridiculous assertion?

So! You have convinced them, my erstwhile friend. Very well. I concede your victory. That old score of ours is quite settled at last. I should have known better than to have resisted you.

So, do with me as you like. I am quite willing to die. The war is nearly over and I have helped to bring victory to France. I confess your accusations. You are quite right. They are all true. I was fighting for my life when I said they weren't. I AM a spy of France. Of course. It is my country. I am not Spanish, as you think, but French. I was a member of the

French secret service when I came to Berlin to dance at the outbreak of the war. My dancing costume was indecently brief for a purpose. My intimacy with you, Herr von Gruttsmacher, was also for a purpose. Could you really imagine that anyone could love you for yourself? You did exactly as I set out to have you do. By admitting me into your service, you enabled me to act without suspicion and under your protection. The valuable information I had from you I took back to France and I sent to you what was purposely misleading.

You will never be able to quite forget me, will you? Always you will have to remember that I was very, very clever and that you were very stupid. Thru you and others like you, I learned what France needed to know.

A courtesan I am—yes. I admit it. But only for the purposes of war. It is a way we women have to confound you men. And it was done to save France and thousands of her brave soldiers!

Immediately? But that is impossible! There is no country in the world that would execute sentence immediately upon its being passed! You must grant me the international privilege of writing some last letters! I am not that dangerous! I have a husband and a little son in Paris. You will, at least, let me communicate with them? No?

Never mind, Padre. Thank you for everything but please do not distress yourself further. The German is ruthless, as always. I understand. I do not blame their hate. I have felt it too.

I die tonight because in France a spy of yours must die. That is the code of war. We do not make it, you and I. And I deserve my death. I die with the death of ten thousand German men on my soul. What does it matter that they were killed in war? My intrigue sent them to their death.

Oh, you men of Germany, do you not see? War, the great madness, has made us all insane! We have all been thru hell in this war. Something horrible entered our hearts—ugly, cruel and fierce. Our souls were not our own. We didn't think of each other then as men but only as the enemy. I have thought it all out these last months, and, now that I am going to die, I am free at last to say what I think. You must listen and try to understand. It is the only light in this darkness.

Surely you can see by now that we must end

this torture. Surely you can understand by now that whoever frees Germany from its rulers frees the people from a suffering that has become the martyrdom of a nation.

I die for no country. I die for a terrible egotism that has butchered the world. I do not mind. Death is, at least, a cure for life.

Padre Casimiro, will you take a message for me to my husband? Send it to the Consul and he will forward it.

Tell him I am not afraid. I am not a child and I am brave. Ask him to raise our boy not in hate nor in revenge. I want him to learn what I could not know before. Teach him that he is part of the whole world—not just one country. Always he will be a son of mine—of our beautiful France—but, more than that, of the world. You understand, my friend, I have seen dreadful things. He must not see what I have—ever. Revenge is bitter to the taste.

That is all. Thank you for everything.

I am ready now. Good-bye.